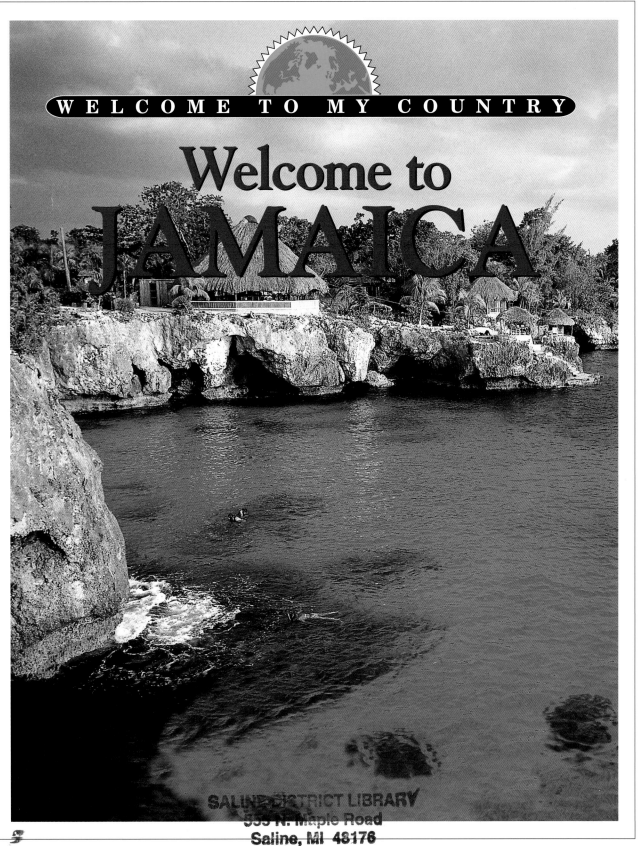

Welcome to JAMAICA

Gareth Stevens Publishing
A WORLD ALMANAC EDUCATION GROUP COMPANY

Written by
KAREN KWEK

Edited by
MELVIN NEO

Edited in USA by
JIM MEZZANOTTE

Designed by
GEOSLYN LIM

Picture research by
SUSAN JANE MANUEL

First published in North America in 2005 by
Gareth Stevens Publishing
A World Almanac Education Group Company
330 West Olive Street, Suite 100
Milwaukee, Wisconsin 53212 USA

Please visit our web site at
www.garethstevens.com
For a free color catalog describing
Gareth Stevens Publishing's list of high-quality
books and multimedia programs,
call 1-800-542-2595 (USA) or
1-800-387-3178 (Canada).
Gareth Stevens Publishing's fax: (414) 332-3567.

© **MARSHALL CAVENDISH INTERNATIONAL (ASIA)
PRIVATE LIMITED 2004**
Originated and designed by
Times Editions Marshall Cavendish
An imprint of Marshall Cavendish International (Asia) Pte Ltd
A member of Times Publishing Limited
Times Centre, 1 New Industrial Road
Singapore 536196
http://www.timesone.com.sg/te

Library of Congress Cataloging-in-Publication Data
Kwek, Karen.
Welcome to Jamaica / Karen Kwek.
p. cm. — (Welcome to my country)
Includes bibliographical references and index.
ISBN 0-8368-2564-0 (lib. bdg.)
1. Jamaica — Juvenile literature. I. Title. II. Series.
F1868.2.K94   2004
972.92—dc22   2004041634

Printed in Singapore

1 2 3 4 5 6 7 8 9 08 07 06 05 04

PICTURE CREDITS
Art Directors and TRIP Photographic Library:
   3 (center and top), 7, 8, 16, 17,
   18 (bottom), 25 (top), 26, 27 (top),
   30 (bottom), 37, 41 (both)
Jan Butchofsky/Houserstock: 25 (bottom)
Steve Cohen/Houserstock: 9
Focus Team — Italy: 10, 20
Getty Images/Hulton Archive: 11, 13, 14,
   15 (bottom), 27 (bottom), 33 (bottom), 35
Haga Library, Japan: cover, 1, 4, 24, 40
David G. Houser/Houserstock: 33 (top)
Hutchison Library: 18 (top), 29
Lynn Seldon: 31, 38
David Simson: 2, 5, 6, 12, 19, 21, 22, 23,
   28, 32, 34, 36, 39
Topham Picturepoint: 15 (top)
Travel Ink: 3 (bottom), 30 (top), 45

Digital Scanning by Superskill Graphics Pte Ltd

Contents

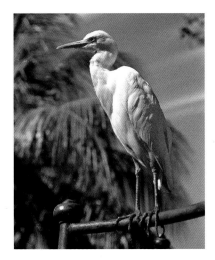

Words that appear in the glossary are printed in **boldface** type the first time they occur in the text.

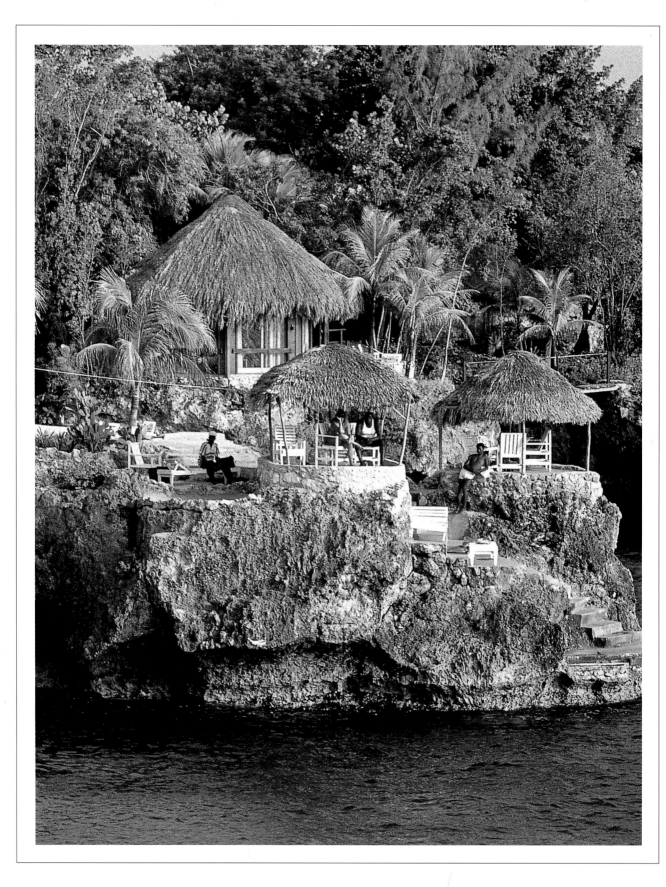

Welcome to Jamaica!

Jamaica is a small island located in the Caribbean Sea. The country is known for its sunny beaches and beautiful mountains, but it also has a history of hardship and struggle. Today, Jamaica has a **diverse** blend of **cultures**. Let's learn more about Jamaica and its people.

Opposite: Jamaica is a great place to enjoy the sea. These beach huts are in Negril, a resort area on the western edge of the island.

Below: A market in Jamaica sells handicrafts made by local people.

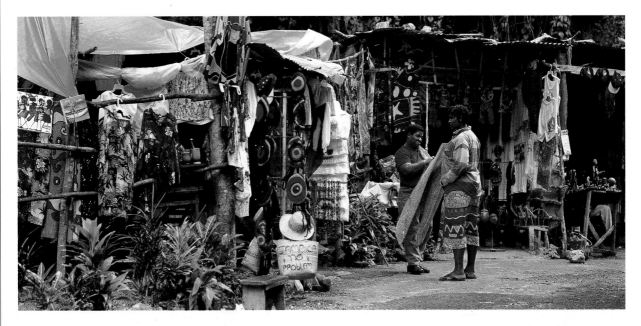

The Flag of Jamaica

The color gold on the Jamaican flag symbolizes wealth and sunlight. Black stands for hardships Jamaicans faced in the past and may meet in the future. Green represents Jamaica's plentiful natural resources and the hope of its people.

5

The Land

Jamaica is part of the Greater Antilles, a chain of islands on the northern edge of the Caribbean Sea. The countries nearest to Jamaica are Cuba to the north and Haiti to the east.

The island of Jamaica has an area of 4,244 square miles (10,992 square kilometers). Jamaica is actually the tip of a mountain that lies mostly beneath the sea's surface. Much of the land consists of mountains and valleys.

Below: Montego Bay is one of Jamaica's main tourist centers.

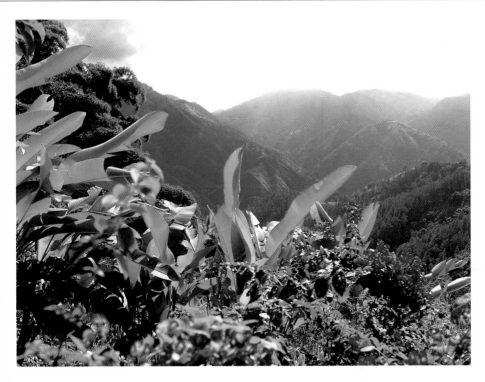

Left: Many rare plants grow in the forests of the Blue Mountains. The world-famous Jamaica Blue Mountain coffee beans also grow on these slopes.

The main mountain range in Jamaica extends east to west along the center of the island. It is often called "the backbone of Jamaica." In the east lie the Blue Mountains and the John Crow Mountains. Dolphin Head, a proposed national park, is in the west.

Parks and Plantations

Jamaica has two national parks, the Blue Mountains-John Crow National Park and Montego Bay Marine Park. It also has many botanical gardens as well as sugar and fruit **plantations**.

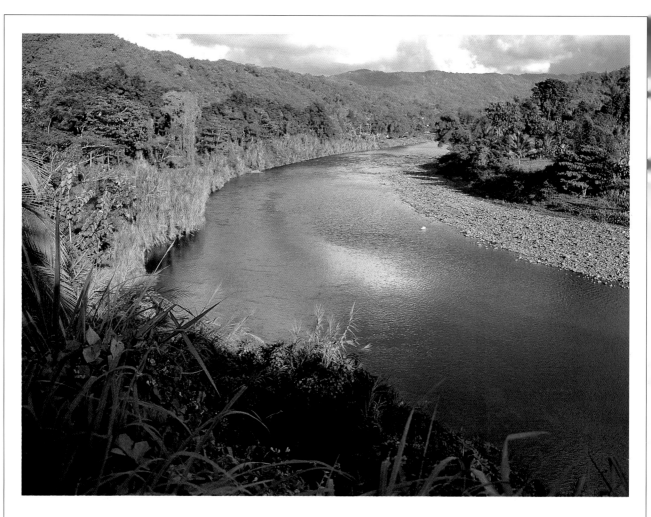

Climate

Jamaica has a mostly warm climate, but temperatures on the island vary. In Kingston, Jamaica's capital, the annual average temperature is 90° Fahrenheit (32° Celsius). At higher **altitudes** in the mountains, temperatures are cooler. The island has two rainy seasons, one in May and another during October and November.

Above: The Rio Grande flows through eastern Jamaica. The island's largest **navigable** river is the Black River. Because Jamaica is so mountainous, most rivers are not navigable.

Plants and Animals

Jamaican plant life includes many species of orchids and ferns. The island's most common mammal is the mongoose. The **endangered** Jamaican hutia, or coney, is a mammal that looks like a guinea pig. Jamaica also has many species of bats, frogs, lizards, and birds. The streamertail hummingbird, the national bird, is also known to locals as "Doctor Bird."

Below: Crocodiles can be found in wetlands and mangrove swamps on the southern coast of Jamaica. More than seven hundred species of fish live in the waters around the island.

History

Before the late 1400s, Jamaica was home to the native *Taino* (tah-EE-no) people. Then, in 1494, Christopher Columbus landed on the island. The Spanish built a **colony** there in 1509. They forced the Taino people to work as slaves on plantations.

By the 1600s, European diseases, hard work, and harsh treatment had wiped out most of the Taino people.

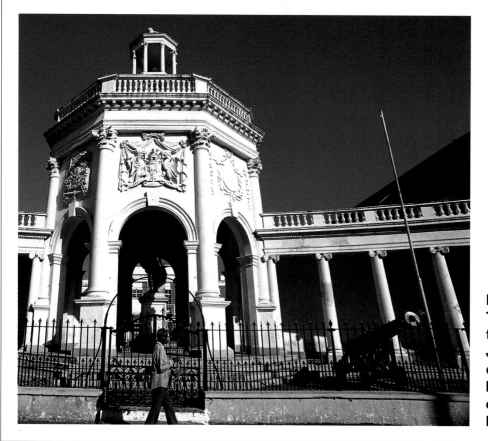

Left: Spanish Town was once the capital of Jamaica. Many of the government buildings in the city are built in a European style.

English Rule

In 1655, the English captured Jamaica from the Spanish. With most of the Taino people gone, the English used **indentured** plantation workers from other Caribbean islands and England. Later, slaves were brought from Africa. In 1838, slaves in Jamaica were freed, and workers were hired from countries such as China and India.

Above:
This illustration shows indentured cotton pickers at work in a cotton field in Jamaica in the 1700s.

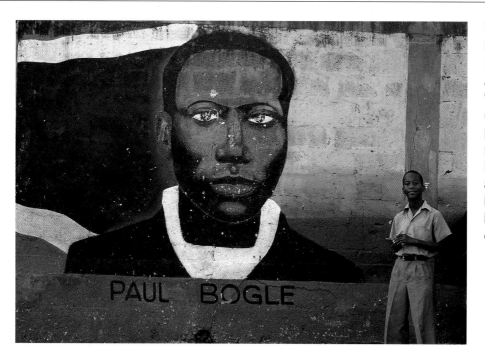

The 1865 Rebellion

After slavery ended, conditions were very bad for Jamaica's black people. White people treated them unfairly. Sugar prices fell, and many people lost their jobs on plantations.

In 1865, farmer Paul Bogle led a group of peasants in a **rebellion** against Jamaica's white rulers. The group marched on the Morant Bay courthouse, where violence broke out. The courthouse caught fire, and several people died. Paul Bogle was hanged for his part in the rebellion.

Political Changes

By the early 1900s, Jamaican workers were forming **trade unions**. Through these groups, workers could ask for higher **wages** and better working conditions. Political parties, such as the People's National Party (PNP) and the Jamaica Labour Party (JLP), were then created to fight for more say in how Jamaica was governed.

In 1944, all adult Jamaicans were given the right to vote. Elections were held that year, and the JLP won.

Below: In this 1962 photograph taken at Buckingham Palace in London, Britain's Queen Elizabeth II (*front row, middle*) poses with leaders from several nations. Alexander Bustamante, the prime minister of Jamaica at the time, stands directly behind the queen.

The Road to Independence

During and after World War II (1939–1945), Jamaicans continued to protest for more control of their government. Jamaica was still a British colony. In 1959, Jamaica was granted full self-government, and PNP leader Norman Manley became prime minister. In 1962, Jamaica gained independence. That same year, Alexander Bustamante became the first prime minister of an independent Jamaica.

Below: Alexander Bustamante (*far left*) and Norman Manley (*far right*) shake hands with British officials after the Jamaica Independence Conference held in 1962.

Mary Jane Seacole (1805–1881)

A highly skilled nurse, Mary Jane Seacole learned traditional healing methods from her mother. When a disease called cholera broke out in the Caribbean islands in 1850, she prepared a cure. She spent her life caring for the sick and injured.

Mary Jane Seacole

Sir Alexander Bustamante (1884–1977)

The first prime minister of an independent Jamaica, Alexander Bustamante established the first Jamaican trade union. He was made a National Hero for his role in freeing Jamaica from British rule.

Dr. Thomas P. Lecky (1904–1994)

Thomas Lecky is best known for creating Jamaica's own breed of cattle, called the "Jamaica Hope." This popular breed produces more milk than other tropical breeds.

Sir Alexander Bustamante

Government and the Economy

The Jamaican government is made up of executive, legislative, and judicial branches. The executive branch has a cabinet of ministers led by a prime minister, who heads the government. The country's legislative branch, the **parliament**, consists of the Senate and the House of Representatives. It creates Jamaica's laws. A system of courts makes up the judicial branch.

Below:
This government building is located in Spanish Town. The city was the capital of Jamaica until 1872, when Kingston became the capital.

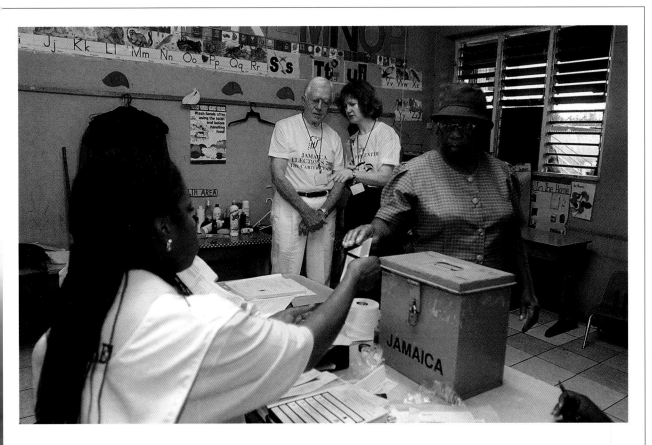

Local Government

Parish councils make up Jamaica's local government. Jamaica has three counties—Cornwall, Middlesex, and Surrey—and it is also divided into fourteen parishes. Every parish is governed by a parish council that handles matters such as public health, garbage collection, and maintenance of roads, parks, and markets. Councils receive money from Jamaica's central government, based in Kingston.

Above: This woman is voting in the Jamaican general elections. Parish council members are elected every three years, and elections for the House of Representatives are held at least once every five years. All Jamaicans aged eighteen and older can vote.

Economy

The economy of Jamaica is healthy compared to other Caribbean nations. Jamaicans do suffer, however, from rising prices and a shortage of jobs.

Jamaica's main industries include tourism, agriculture, and mining. A large number of Jamaicans work in tourism-related jobs. The country's main crops are sugar, bananas, citrus fruits, cocoa, coconuts, and **pimento** (allspice). Mines in Jamaica produce bauxite, a substance that is used to make the metal aluminum.

Above: Young banana plants are carefully grown at this nursery. Most of the banana plantations in Jamaica are on the eastern side of the island.

Left: Formed in 1969, Air Jamaica plays a key role in the Jamaican tourist industry. Tourism is an important part of Jamaica's economy.

Trade

Jamaica trades mainly with the United States, the United Kingdom and other European nations, and Canada. The country's **imports** include finished goods and raw materials. Its **exports** include crops and bauxite.

Getting Around

Most people travel around Jamaica by car, bus, or airplane. The island has two international airports and four domestic, or local, airports.

Above: Buses are a common form of transportation in Jamaica.

People and Lifestyle

Jamaicans are **descendants** of people from many different cultures. Before slavery ended in 1838, West African slaves and Europeans came to the island. After 1838, Chinese, East Indians, and more Europeans arrived.

Today, Jamaica has a population of more than 2.6 million people. At least another 2 million Jamaicans live in other countries all over the world.

Below: Many people visit the markets along the streets of Montego Bay.

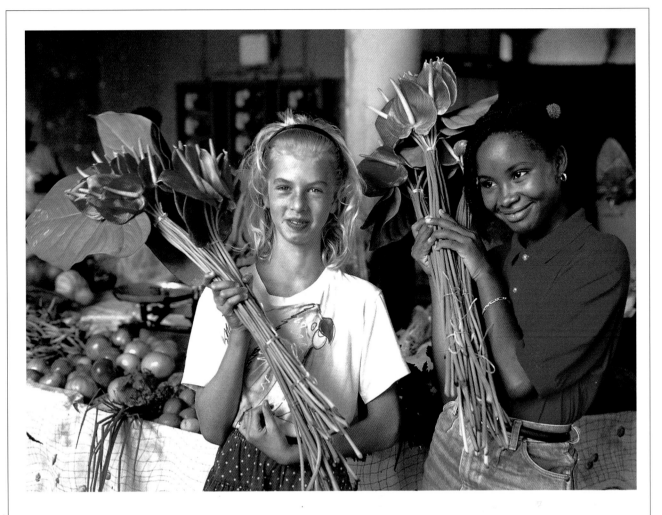

Jamaica's motto—"Out of Many, One People"—describes the way different kinds of people live together in Jamaica, creating a unique blend of cultures. More than 90 percent of Jamaicans are of African descent, and 7.3 percent are of mixed parentage. The island is also home to East Indians, Chinese, Jews, and whites descended from European indentured workers.

Above: Children of different races study and play together every day in Jamaica. The **constitution** of Jamaica gives all racial groups the same rights.

City and Country Living

Kingston is the capital of Jamaica. It is the center of government, business, and culture on the island, and it is steadily growing. Many people live in Kingston. Others travel there every day to work.

In the countryside, many families are extremely poor. Most people work on farms. They may own their own farms or work on other people's farms. Some people have jobs in mining or tourism.

Below: This shack is in Cockpit Country. Some parts of the Jamaican countryside do not have proper housing, schools, or public services.

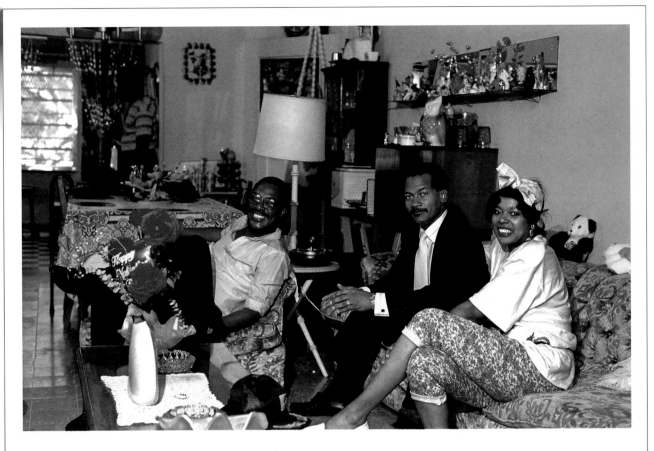

Family Life

Jamaica has many kinds of families. Some families consist of two parents and children, while others consist of one parent and children. In recent years, the number of single mothers has risen. Jamaica also has extended families, with parents, children, and other relatives living together. Many parents go to the United States or England to find work, leaving their children with relatives or guardians.

Above: Families in Jamaica often spend Sundays together at home after they go to church. On the island, most fathers play a smaller role in raising children than mothers do.

23

Education

In the past, few Jamaicans received a decent education. Today, however, 85 percent of Jamaicans aged fifteen and older can read and write.

Children in Jamaica start school at age three. They usually spend two years in kindergarten and six years in primary school. They attend high school for five years. Some students continue their education at one of the universities on the island.

Below:
These Jamaican primary-school students are enjoying a recess break. In Jamaica, students begin high school at age eleven or twelve.

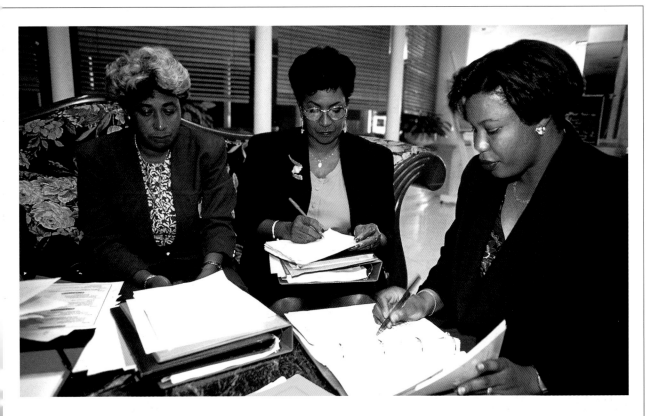

Women in Jamaica

Women play many important roles in Jamaica. Most Jamaican women are very independent, and many of them are single mothers who must support their families. Although the Jamaican government does not have many women leaders, more women than men work in Jamaica. Most of the country's teachers are women. A high percentage of women in Jamaica can read and write, and more women than men attend Jamaica's universities.

Above: In Jamaica, women are an important part of the workforce.

Below: This woman in Jamaica sells flowers and fruit.

Religion

Christianity came to Jamaica in the 1500s when the Spanish introduced Roman Catholicism. Later, the English brought **Protestant** beliefs. Today, more than 65 percent of Jamaicans are Christian, and most of these Christians are Protestants. The Church of God is the largest Protestant group. Other Protestant groups include Baptists, Anglicans, Seventh-Day Adventists, and Pentecostalists.

Below: North Street Cathedral in Kingston is one of many churches in Jamaica. Churches are centers of social life in Jamaican communities.

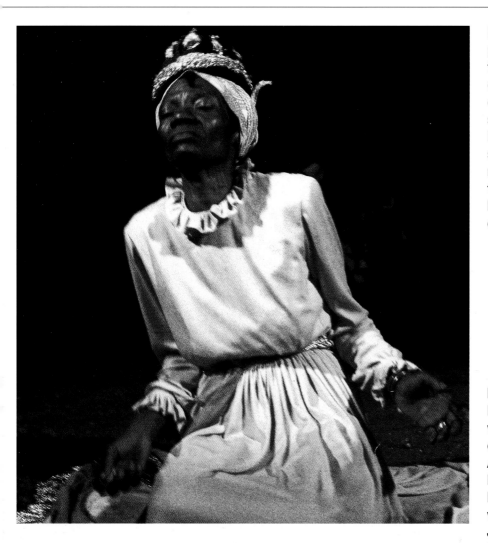

Left: A Kumina priestess moves to drumbeats and chanting. Followers of Kumina believe spirits can be found in natural objects such as trees and rocks, and that these spirits can be persuaded to do good or evil.

Below: Haile Selassie was the ruler of Ethiopia, an African country. Followers of Rastafarianism, which began in Jamaica, believe Selassie is a savior of black people and the king of all Africa.

Almost 35 percent of Jamaicans are followers of non-Christian religions, which include Judaism, Islam, Hinduism, Rastafarianism, and traditional African beliefs. *Pocomania* (poh-koh-MAY-nee-ah) and *Kumina* (koo-MEE-nah) are traditional Jamaican religions that have African roots.

Language

The official language of Jamaica is English. In everyday conversation, however, many people in Jamaica speak Jamaican *patois* (pa-TWAH). This patois is a mixture of Creole English (spoken by British settlers in Jamaica), the African languages of slaves, and Spanish and Portuguese words. Schools in Jamaica used to discourage students from using this patois, but it is now recognized as the country's second language.

Below:
Most Jamaican newspapers and official documents, as well as many books, are written in standard British English. Jamaican patois, however, is more widely spoken than standard English.

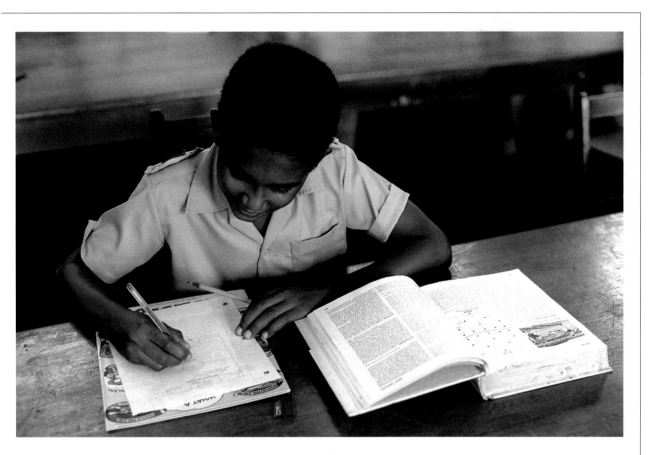

Literature

Jamaican literature began to **flourish** in the 1960s when Jamaica gained independence. Some Jamaicans wrote about the problems of British rule, including slavery. Other Jamaicans, such as Louise Bennett-Coverley, wrote about everyday life on the island. Coverley and other writers also explored the use of Jamaican patois, helping it to become better accepted by people in Jamaica.

Above: In Jamaican schools, students read the works of many Jamaican writers. These works include the poems and stories of Louise Bennett-Coverley, who is known as "Miss Lou."

Arts

Jamaica has a wide variety of arts, including music, dance, drama, and visual arts. The National Gallery in Kingston is a good place to explore the country's visual arts. It houses Jamaica's largest collection of historical and contemporary art and features the works of many well-known Jamaican sculptors, painters, and potters.

Above: A potter works on his latest creation.

Pottery is the oldest of Jamaican arts. The island's first potters were the native Taino people, who used red clay to make cooking pots and other items.

Left: The National Gallery in Kingston displays the works of many well-known Jamaican artists, such as potter Cecil Baugh and sculptor Edna Manley.

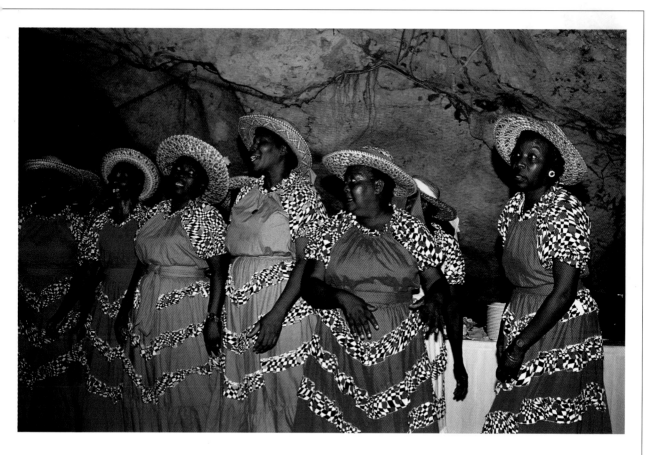

Dance

Jamaicans love to dance. Traditional dance forms in Jamaica have strong African roots. They include Myal, Revival, Quadrille, and Maypole. Modern Jamaican dance is a mixture of traditional dance forms, European classical ballet, and modern dance styles from the United States. The most important dance company in the country is the National Dance Theatre Company.

Above:
In Jamaica, dances are often performed for tourists. These dances showcase the rich history of dance on the island.

Theater

Jamaican theater groups perform a wide range of works. Many performances mix standard theatrical forms, such as drama and comedy, with the acting, singing, and dancing of Jamaican folk theater. Performances also combine standard English and Jamaican patois.

Some theater groups, such as the ASHE Performing Arts Ensemble, use the performing arts to address social problems in Jamaica. This ensemble mostly consists of young Jamaicans.

Below: Kingston's Ward Theatre is a well-known playhouse in Jamaica. Many theater groups are based in Kingston.

Left: Jamaican folk singers often use banjos and maracas.

Music

Jamaica has traditional and popular styles of music. Traditional music has roots in the folk music of African slaves. It is often played on special occasions. Reggae is the most famous popular music in Jamaica. It followed other popular styles, such as mento, ska, and rock steady. In the 1970s, reggae musicians such as Bob Marley began having international success. A form of reggae called dancehall is now popular with young Jamaicans.

Below: Jamaican reggae star Bob Marley made fans around the world with his unique music. He often sang about hope and freedom. He died in 1981.

Leisure

Jamaicans like to spend their free time in groups—the bigger, the better! They enjoy sports and games such as dominoes. Jamaicans also like to go to music festivals. Reggae Sumfest is one of the most exciting music festivals on the island. Every year, it brings together reggae fans from Jamaica and many other parts of the world.

Below:
These young Jamaicans are enjoying a day in Kingston. From shopping malls to cinemas to the most popular dance clubs, Kingston's many attractions draw crowds of young people to the city.

Many Jamaicans enjoy going to the movies. Sometimes, they may see their own country on the screen, because Jamaica is a favorite setting for filmmakers. Several local movies have been made in Jamaica. The first Jamaican-made movie seen by audiences worldwide was *The Harder They Come* in 1973. It stars Jamaican musician Jimmy Cliff and is famous for its reggae soundtrack.

Above: Jamaican-born actress Grace Jones (*far right*) starred with Tanya Roberts (*far left*) and Roger Moore (*center*) in the 1985 James Bond film *A View to a Kill.*

Sports

Sports are a big part of leisure in Jamaica. Soccer, **cricket**, basketball, and netball, a game that is similar to basketball, are popular sports on the island. The Jamaican women's netball team is ranked one of the best in the world. In 1998, the national soccer team reached the World Cup finals for the first time. Jamaicans also like to watch horse racing.

Below: Jamaicans of all ages enjoy beach soccer.

Jamaican Champions

Jamaican athletes have excelled at track and field, becoming Olympic medalists and world champions. At the 1980 Olympic Games, sprinter Merlene Ottey became the first Jamaican female athlete to win an Olympic medal. More recently, Greg Haughton won two bronze medals for Jamaica at the 2000 Olympic Games.

Above: *The Athlete*, a sculpture by Alvin Marriott, stands near the National Stadium in Kingston.

Holidays and Festivals

Jamaica has ten public holidays each year, including Christian holidays such as Christmas and Easter. The island also has several festivals.

Emancipation Day is the first day of August. This holiday marks the date when slaves in Jamaica were officially freed. Independence Day, on August 6, marks the date when Jamaica became an independent nation.

Below: These local women are performing a folk dance as part of Independence Day celebrations in Jamaica.

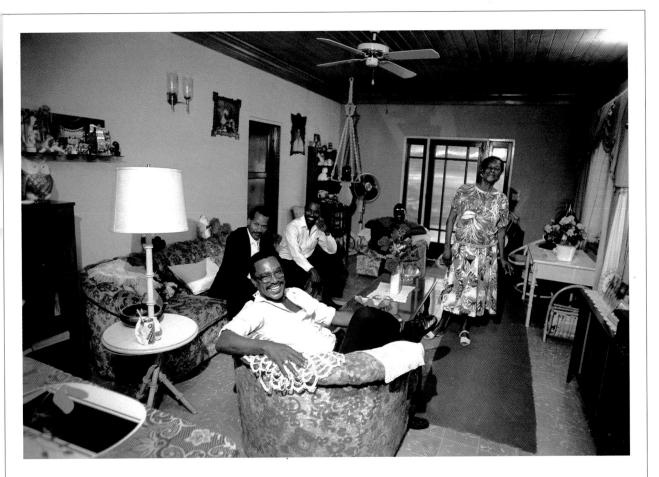

The Jamaica Festival is a mixture of exhibitions and competitions in music, dance, and other arts. Held in summer, the festival takes place throughout the island. Thousands of Jamaicans of all ages help prepare for the festival.

National Heritage Week is held in October and includes National Heroes Day, a public holiday. Events during the week celebrate Jamaican culture and the achievements of Jamaicans.

Above: In Jamaica, holidays are a time when many families relax together at home.

Food

Traditional Jamaican food uses a lot of seasonings, including salt, black pepper, pimento, garlic, onions, and hot peppers. The national dish, ackee and saltfish, combines ackee, a fruit, with heavily salted cod. It is usually a breakfast dish and is often served on Sundays with other foods, such as yams or dumplings. Other traditional foods are hardough (a heavy, white bread) and fried bammies (flat cakes made from **cassava**).

Left: The bright red ackee fruit is poisonous when unripe. When ripe, the fruit opens up. The yellow flesh inside can then be cooked and eaten.

Jerk meat is another Jamaican food. This dish is made from pork, chicken, or fish. First, the meat is **marinated** in herbs and spices. Then, it is wrapped in leaves and slowly cooked over a fire of pimento wood. Jamaican jerk meat is also sold in other countries.

The dishes of other cultures can also be found in Jamaica. Chinese and East Indian workers brought their own foods, cooking styles, and seasonings to the island. The East Indians, for example, introduced a dish called curry goat that is very popular.

Below: Jamaica has a lot of tropical fruits, which are often used to make delicious desserts. Some fruits, such as coconuts, are not native to the island. They were brought to Jamaica from other parts of the world.

A   B   C   D

1

Montego Bay

● **Montego Bay**

HANOVER

Dolphin Head

ST. JAMES

TRELAWNY

C O R N W A L L

2

Negril

WESTMORELAND

The Cockpit Country

ST. ANN

M I D D L E S

Black River

ST. ELIZABETH

MANCHESTER

CLARENDON

ST. CATHERINE

Spanish To

Rio Cobre

Rio Minho

3

C A R I B B E A N   S E A

4

JAMAICA

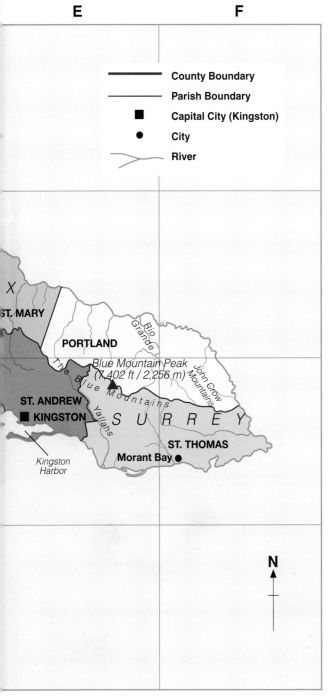

Black River
B2–B3
Blue Mountain
Peak E3
Blue Mountains
E3–F3

Caribbean Sea
A4–F4
Clarendon C2–D4
Cockpit Country
B2–C3
Cornwall A2–C3

Dolphin Head B2

Hanover A2–B2

John Crow
Mountains F3

Kingston E3
Kingston Harbor
D3–E3

Manchester
C2–C3

Middlesex C2–D3
Montego Bay B2
Morant Bay F3

Negril A2

Portland E2–F3

Rio Grande E2–F3
Rio Cobre D3

St. Andrew D2–E3
St. Ann C2–D2
St. Catherine
D2–D3
St. Elizabeth
B2–C3
St. James B1–B2
St. Mary D2–E2
St. Thomas E3–F3
Spanish Town D3
Surrey E2–F3

Trelawny B1–C2

Westmoreland
A2–B3

Quick Facts

Official Name   Jamaica

Capital   Kingston

Main Languages   English (official), Jamaican patois

Population   2,695,867 (2003 estimate)

Land Area   4,244 square miles (10,992 square km)

Counties   Cornwall, Middlesex, Surrey

Parishes   Clarendon, Hanover, Kingston, Manchester, Portland, St. Andrew, St. Ann, St. Catherine, St. Elizabeth, St. James, St. Mary, St. Thomas, Trelawny, Westmoreland

Highest Point   Blue Mountain Peak 7,402 feet (2,256 m)

Major Rivers   Black River, Rio Cobre, Rio Grande

Main Religion   Christianity

Major Holidays   Good Friday (March/April)
Easter (March/April)
Emancipation Day (August 1)
Independence Day (August 6)
Christmas (December 25)

Currency   Jamaican Dollar (JMD 60.10 = U.S. $1 in 2004)

Opposite: The white egret is one of many bird species found in Jamaica.

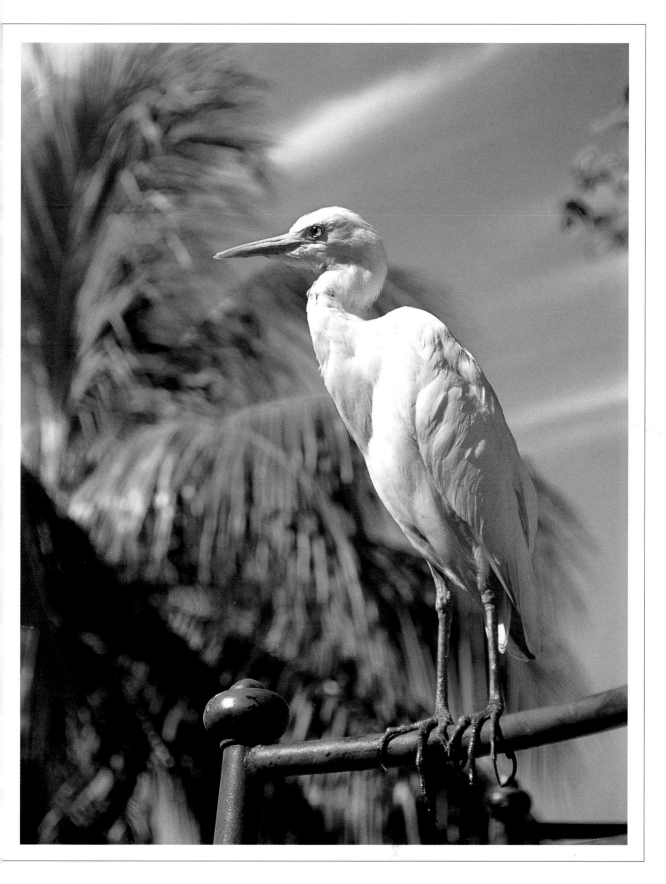

Glossary

altitudes: heights above sea level.

cassava: a kind of plant with a root that can be cooked and eaten.

colony: an area that is settled and governed by another country.

constitution: a set of laws establishing how a country is governed and the rights of the people.

cricket: a game played with a ball and bat on a large field by two sides, with each side usually consisting of eleven players.

cultures: the sets of customs, beliefs, language, literature, and art belonging to particular peoples or countries.

descendants: the later generations of particular families.

diverse: having many differences and much variety.

endangered: in danger of dying out completely, or becoming extinct.

exports: goods sent out of a country to be sold in another country.

flourish: grow or develop quickly and successfully.

imports: goods from other countries that are brought into a country to be sold there.

indentured: having signed an agreement to work for a person for a period of time, often in return for the payment of transportation and other costs.

marinated: soaked in something, such as seasonings, before being cooked.

navigable: suitable for travel by boat.

parliament: an official government body of elected representatives who make the laws of their country.

patois: the special language of a certain group of people.

pimento: the berry of the pimento tree, which is often dried and used as a seasoning and is also called allspice.

plantations: large farms, which usually have many workers.

Protestant: part of a particular group of Christian faiths that differ from Roman Catholicism.

rebellion: organized opposition to a government or other authority.

Taino: the native people of islands in the Caribbean Sea.

trade unions: organizations of workers that try to improve wages, benefits, and working conditions for members.

wages: the money workers receive.

More Books to Read

Doctor Bird: Three Lookin' Up Tales from Jamaica. Gerald Hausman (Philomel Books)

I Am a Rastafarian. Religions of the World series. Jane Stuart (Powerkids Press)

Jamaica. Michael Capek (Carolrhoda Books)

Jamaica. Discovering the Caribbean series. Colleen Madonna Flood Williams (Mason Crest Publishers)

Jamaica. Festivals of the World series. Robert Barlas (Gareth Stevens)

Jamaica. True Books series. Ann Heinrichs (Children's Press)

Jamaica. We Come from series. Alison Brownlie (Raintree)

Jamaica the People. Lands, Peoples, and Cultures series. Amber Wilson (Crabtree Publishing)

Videos

Jamaica. AAA Travel Video series. (International Video)

Jamaica: Land of Wood and Water. (Library Video)

Jamaica Experience. (Questar)

Travels in Mexico and the Caribbean: Jamaica, Miami, and the Bahamas. (Questar)

Web Sites

http://nature.org/wherewework/ caribbean/jamaica

www.elmuseo.org/taino

www.jnht.com

www.nlj.org.jm/docs/ heroes_emblems.htm

Due to the dynamic nature of the Internet, some web sites stay current longer than others. To find additional web sites, use a reliable search engine with one or more of the following keywords to help you locate information about Jamaica: *Bob Marley, dancehall music, John Crow Mountains, Kingston, reggae, Spanish Town, Taino.*

Index